THE TERRIBLE SHEARS

THE
TERRIBLE SHEARS

SCENES FROM
A TWENTIES CHILDHOOD

By
D. J. Enright

1973
CHATTO & WINDUS
LONDON

Published by
Chatto & Windus Ltd
42 William IV Street
London W.C.2

★

Clarke, Irwin & Co. Ltd
Toronto

ISBN 0 7011 1965 9

ᴄᴄ

Printed in Great Britain by
T. and A. Constable Ltd
Hopetoun Street, Edinburgh

To
MY MOTHER

LITTLE BUDDHAS

We had to keep our coal out at the back;
They wouldn't give us a bath.

I wondered why the Lotus Position seemed familiar—
It was how we crouched in the copper on bath night.

USES OF LITERACY

When not in use, the copper
Was lined with old newspapers.
I was an early reader
(The one art that costs no money),
I could read upside-down—

Adverts for objects of
Unimaginable use, or the
News of the great world.
We didn't expect to understand
Such things.

THE NIGHTS

Unsure in summer,
You lie in bed in the light and feel you must be
Sick. Sheet lightning spoils the later night.

Safer in winter,
The oilstove throws its gently trembling patterns
On the wall. Accord of warmth and light and night.

NIGHT-LIGHT

In childhood there was this dream,
Recurrent and unyielding—
I was in a dark mill, or I was the mill,
The grindstones were grinding, with nothing
At all to grind, they groaned and groaned,
And when I woke, the dull heavy sound
Went on. I would wait for it to stop.
But in the end I had to call my mother.

GROWING UP

I came to know this later dream
Like the two-times-table.
          I was crossing
The Suspension Bridge. When I
Got halfway, I dropped to the ground,
Shrank paper-thin and slipped between
The rails. The water rose to meet me.
As I hit it, I woke.

"Soon be over," I told myself, as I
Began to fall. Then as I neared the spot.
Then "Soon be over," I said, as soon as
The dream began. I was getting too old
To call for my mother.

MINORITIES

In the early Fifties we were the only
Foreign family in the hamlet of Okamoto.
At times an old crone would recoil
In the market, a baby howl with terror.
But the natives were very kind to us.

In my childhood there was only one
Black family in Leamington.
The natives were kind to them,
They were better-behaved than the Irish.

RESPECTED MEMBERS OF THE COMMUNITY

Mind you, this blackie was a postman;
As was my father, a mick.
Postmen were saintly figures in those days.
They were paid with cups of tea and kindly words.

TWO BAD THINGS IN INFANT SCHOOL

Learning bad grammar, then getting blamed for it:
Learning Our Father which art in Heaven.

Bowing our heads to a hurried nurse, and
Hearing the nits rattle down on the paper.

AND TWO GOOD THINGS

Listening to Miss Anthony, our lovely Miss,
Charming us dumb with *The Wind in the Willows*.

Dancing Sellinger's Round, and dancing and
Dancing it, and getting it perfect forever.

BUT ONCE A YEAR

The cracked oilcloth is hidden
By a knife-creased tablecloth.
On it bottles of Vimto squat,
A few flakes of browning tinsel
Settle. It is Christmas—
Someone will pay for this.

JINGLE BELLS

Our presents were hidden on top of the cupboard.
Climbing up, we found a musical box, in the shape
Of a roller, which you pushed along the floor.

This was for our new sister, she was only
A few months old, her name was Valerie.

Just before Christmas (this I know is a memory
For no one ever spoke of it) the baby quietly
Disgorged a lot of blood, and was taken away.

The musical box disappeared too,
As my sister and I noted with mixed feelings.
We were not too old to play with it.

11

A GLIMPSE

She was bending over the kitchen sink,
Milk, warm and unwanted, draining away,
Milk mingling with tears—or so I now think.

WHERE DID DAD SPEND CHRISTMAS?

Christmas was always a bad time.
My father was on country delivery,
And either he broke his wrist when
Swinging the engine, or the van skidded
Into a ditch with him inside it.

(Once he only suffered from shock.
He ran over a large dog—"it lifted the van
Clean off the ground"—but looking back,
He could see nothing on the road but snow.)

The hours passed, and there was no sign
Of Dad. "We'll let you know as soon as
We hear anything," said the kindly Post Office.
We began to think he was Father Christmas.

ANOTHER CHRISTMAS

Another Christmas was coming.
Father thought of a way of enriching it for us.
He recalled that on the Somme
He had carried from the battlefield
A wounded officer by the name of Crawford.

(It was now a household name.)

He wrote to the gentleman in question,
Mentioning the not so distant incident
And the coming of Christmas. In return
There came a free packet of assorted biscuits.

They were consumed, and no doubt enjoyed,
Though felt to be less than they might have been.

LITTLE ANGELS

Look through those family albums:
Each one contains a paradox.

Among recurrent characters
In careful suits and frocks
Or jacketless and jolly—
Sudden, unaccountable,
An alien apparition.

My mother, she could show a creature
Rosy in lace and velvet,
By-blow of some queer artist.
"A little angel!" Yes indeed.
I wouldn't have been safe on the street.

Where did all that finery go?
What became of those smug pretties?
They make their one appearance,
Then the Box Brownies take the lot.
Did the plague of Egypt wipe them out?

Somewhere there'll be a picture of him,
My idiot cousin,
Looking like the baby Plato
Or Infant Jesus.

EARLY DISCOVERY

My sense of the superiority of women
Was confirmed at the age of seven.

My young sister was leaning against
The cast-iron railings of the balcony of
The third-floor room in which we lived.
The railings began to fall into the street,
The child began to follow.

My father and I were transfixed.
My mother, though hampered by a bread knife in the
    right hand,
Flew out and pulled the child back with the left.

Then my father had to go down and apologize
To a man in the street whom the cast iron had just missed.

ANGLO-IRISH

My father claimed to be descended from a king
Called Brian Boru, an ancient hero of Ireland.

My mother said that all Irishmen claimed descent
From kings but the truth was they were Catholics.

We would have preferred to believe our father.
Experience had taught us to trust in our mother.

JEPHSON GARDENS

Two small children in the Gardens on Sunday,
Playing quietly at husband and wife.

How sweet, says an old lady, as she sits on
The bench: you must surely be brother and sister?

No, says the boy, we are husband and wife.
How sweet, says the old lady: but really you are
Brother and sister, aren't you now, really?

No, says the boy, trapped in his fantasy,
I am the husband, she is the wife.

The old lady moves off, she doesn't like liars,
She says. She doesn't think we are sweet any longer.

FLOWERS

The town was proud of the town's gardens,
People came from all over to view them.
I was taken there on Thursday afternoons
Or Sundays, when admission was free.

You couldn't play games in the Jephson Gardens,
Except for miniature golf at sixpence a round.

The aesthetic sense lay stillborn in me,
Those masses of flowers did nothing to me.

Later, having reached the Pathetic Fallacy,
I looked at them more closely: they were emblematic
Of something, I couldn't make out what.

On Sundays those masses of flowers pressed round me,
Muttering, muttering too softly for me to hear.
Their language, in my inept translation,
Was thick with portentous clichés.

I never learnt their true names.
If I looked at them now,
I would only see the sound of Sunday church bells.

UNCLE JACK

Though all that time he never left the house
Uncle Jack got more and more weatherbeaten.
He was crippled with rheumatics
From building bridges over rivers.

He was the bad-tempered uncle,
His smoke-stained cottage the ogre's castle.

Next to bridges, milk was his favourite rage.
He wouldn't take a drop of it, he had worked
On a farm, he knew what went on there.
Uncle Jack on milk wasn't fit for kiddies.

FIRE AND WATER

The canal was nearby, the cut we called it.
A sullen water, it refused to bear away
What we had given it. It gave us back dead eels.
All the sickness of the town lay there.
As I grew up, I came to hate all water.

Over our garden wall the railway embankment
Rose steeply. In summer the grass caught fire.
At an upstairs window, with Granma,
I watched the flames, pale and fierce and quick.
Fire was my favourite element.

THEY: EARLY HORROR FILM

Our pipes froze last winter
Because THEY took all the heat out of the air.

Not but what THEY are more to be avoided
Than envied.

Remember what THEY did to Joe Walters down the road—
Mucked him about properly.

THEY put Tom Binns in prison for stealing registered letters,
THEY drove up in their Sunbeams and caught him in the act.

THEY're a funny lot, but clever with it.
THEIR maker gave them fancies and the means to gratify
    them.

THEY drink blood after saying grace in Latin.

That Mrs Tooms opposite is stuck-up: she sits at
Her window drinking blood from a teacup, but I bet
She doesn't know any Latin.
Latin isn't for the likes of Mrs Tooms,
Nor is blood.
Even if her son is doing well in the Town Clerk's at
    Folkestone,
Or so she says.

Sometimes THEY try to get round you,
THEY come bearing scholarships.

Keep out of THEIR way, child!
Nothing but shame and sorrow follow.

The divel! Here THEY are, at the door—
Don't open it till I've put something decent on.

"Yes sir, no sir,
We wouldn't know anything about that, sir."

THEY didn't get anything out of *me*!

SHADES OF THE PRISON HOUSE

How many remember that nightmare word
The Workhouse? It was like a black canal
Running through our lives.

"Old Mrs Povey has gone to the Workhouse."
"You'll end in the Workhouse if you go on like that."

It was shameful to end in the Workhouse.
Shameful to have a relative in the Workhouse,
The worst shame of all.
Such shame was always possible.

Even children came to dread the Workhouse.
Other times, other bogy men.

PATIENCE

Patience was another potent word.
Patience was a virtue—in effect
It seemed to be the only one.

Certainly a virtue for virtue's sake,
There wasn't the slightest suggestion
It would lead to anything beyond
A respectable death, the undertaker paid.

Patience was our favourite game.
My mother is still addicted to it.

The word used to make us mad—
Patience, patience all day long!
Getting mad would lead to breaking plates
Or tearing one's clothes, that was all.

(And when we were short of cash
Who was the one to go short of food?
The patient one.)

Putting up with things
Was a speciality of the age.
You couldn't change things, and
Trying to would only make you miserable.

Nowadays clothes are manufactured torn,
There's hardly any china left.

It's not surprising that these days
No one puts up with anything, and
Patience is the rarest of words, and
Change the most vulgar.

HAPPINESS

Yes, of course there were happy times,
It was not a succession of disasters.

(Once we went to Weston-super-Mare: the sea
Had apparently retreated to Leamington.)

The happiness you must take as read,
The writing of it is so difficult.

PLAYING

As kids we had great fun
With my granpa's Bath chair, till
He came shouting to chase us away.

In Siam I watched urchins
Playing about a pedicab, till
The driver chased them away with curses.

A lowering way of earning one's rice;
For children a treasure trove.

DOLLS

Rag dolls came first; they had
Good characters.
       The best character of all
Was Golly.

In my sister's time there were
The baby dolls with idiot faces.
They had real eyes and things.
They could twist their arms and legs
In unnatural ways.
You couldn't play house with such,
You had given birth to monsters.

Even when they were dented and
Dirtied it wasn't much better.

WORLD PICTURE

The natural order has it that
Mother is in the house
And father is out of it.

No good comes of them both
Being in the house.
       Either they flirt in a
Queasy fashion. Or they quarrel.
Or one of them is sick.

We were firm believers in the natural order.

SPLENDOUR IN THE GRASS

The eyes of childhood are too keen.
Urban grass is meagre, but the soil
Is rich in worms.

("Don't call it *dirt,* dear child!"
Cried Henry James. But call it what?)

If I were a Committee
I'd try to prevent children from playing
With slugs and snails and worms.

So young to play in open graves—
Couldn't that come later?

FACTS OF LIFE

I had two white mice—
Then I had scores of baby mice,
Naked and pink little things, dead or
Alive or half-eaten.

Those two small mice did me more harm
Than all the pornography in the world.
My father took them away.

The dog went too.
Him we liked. But he was a creature
Of the open spaces, he needed
Long hours of exercise in the park.

He went back to the country. I hope
That was where he went.

WAR GAME

When the soldiers lost their limbs
They were turned to wounded soldiers

Put to nursing, a farmyard milkmaid
Carried in her pails the limbs of soldiers

A section of the rails was missing: here
The track blew up, hurting the soldiers

A general might have to ride a hippo
Commandeered from Noah's Ark

A wooden tiger carry off the wounded
The milkmaid and her pails as well

The more things went to pot
The more authentic the whole thing got.

RUDE HEALTH

Brimstone and treacle (not bad that),
Powders disguised in strawberry jam
(Even now I can't touch strawberry jam),
California Syrup of Figs and Parrish's Food,
Senna tea (it spoilt me for the Chinese kind),
Cascara sagrada (which I now perceive
Bears a most impressive etymology),
And something peculiarly horrible
Which we should have been given more often
Except that no one could pronounce its name—
Ipecacuanha Wine.

Such the incessant medication of our childhood.

Since when I have needed nothing beyond an
Occasional aspirin.

YOUNG CRIMINALS

"The same to you with knobs on," said the first.
"The same to you with spikes on," said the second.
"The same to you with balls on," said the third.

The master heard us. He was a just man.
The first of us got one stroke on each hand.
I got two strokes on each hand.
The third got a fearful beating—
He was a dunce, he smelt, his name was Bugg.

(About the time I left Clapham Terrace Elementary
He was put away for showing his thing in the street.)

TRAINING

How docile we were, how orderly! Empire Day,
Armistice Day, and all that religious instruction!
They were training us to die for something—
It meant nothing, only holidays and queer emotions.

Forty years later, walking in Canton, I encounter
A mass of orderly children—they are listening
Intently, with every sign of agreement,
To a horror story about red-haired imperialists.

I slope past fearfully. But to them I'm no more
Than a comical flower in this well-kept park.
Keeping one's eyes on teacher is far more important.
As yet they haven't learnt to connect.

A SIGN

At an early age I achieved a sort of
Puzzled fame in the family circle.

I retrieved an old broken-backed
Bible from the dustbin and bore it
Back into the house. No doubt
With a scandalized look on my face
Though not wishful to chide these
Blasphemers against God's Word.

At that tender age I couldn't bear
To see printed matter ill treated.
I would have subscribed to the ancient
Oriental taboo against stepping light-
Mindedly over paper inscribed with characters.

It was read as a sign. The child
Is destined to become Vicar of the Parish Church!
He has rescued Religion from the scrap-heap.

Now I could watch unmoved the casting
Of hundreds of books into dustbins.
But two of them I think I should still
Dive in after—Shakespeare and the Bible.

SUNDAY

My mother's strongest religious feeling
Was that Catholics were a sinister lot;
She would hardly trust even a lapsed one.
My father was a lapsed Catholic.

Yet we were sent to Sunday school.
Perhaps in the spirit that others
Were sent to public schools. It
Might come in useful later on.

In Sunday school a sickly adult
Taught the teachings of a sickly lamb
To a gathering of sickly children.

It was a far cry from that brisk person
Who created the heaven and the earth in
Six days and then took Sunday off.

The churches were run by a picked crew
Of bad actors radiating insincerity.
Not that one thought of them in that way,
One merely disliked the sound of their voices.
I cannot recall one elevated moment in church,
Though as a choirboy I pulled in a useful
Sixpence per month.

Strange, that a sense of religion should
Somehow survive all this grim buffoonery!
Perhaps that brisk old person does exist,
And we are living through his Sunday.

UNCERTAINTIES

Our folk didn't have much
In the way of lore.

But I remember a story,
A warning against envy
And also against good fortune,
Too much for our small heads—

About a lucky man called Jim
(My uncle in Dublin I used to think,
But he was Sunny Jim)
And his friend who envied him.
Jim had the luck
He married the girl they both of them loved
And his friend envied him.
Then Jim died, and the friend
Married his widow. And then
The friend envied lucky Jim,
Asleep in peace in the churchyard.

When Granpa wasn't pushing old ladies
Through the streets of the Spa
He would cut the grass on selected graves.
Sometimes we went with him. Dogs
Had done their business on the hummocks.
The water smelt bad in the rusty vases.
The terrible shears went clack clack.

It was too much for our small heads.
Who was it that we mustn't envy—
The living or the dead?

THE PICTURES

Threepence on Saturday afternoons,
A bench along the side of the hall—
We looked like Egyptian paintings,
But less composed.

Sometimes a film that frightened us
And returned at nights.
Once *Noah's Ark*, an early talkie
We took for non-fiction.

Cheapest was the home kino.
Lying in bed, you pressed on your eyes,
Strange happenings ensued.

But the story was hard to follow
And your eyeballs might fall in.
Fatigued, you fell asleep.

SPOILT

How well we were catered for!
No wonder we lost our teeth.
Chewy locust, thick strong liquorice sticks,
Aniseed balls, bull's-eyes, and sherbet . . .

Later in my prime, at elegant parties in the
Orient (but where was the sherbet? Where
The locust?), I met caviare and smoked salmon
And various oriental delicacies.

They were no sort of substitute.
But happily I found a new strong taste,
Easy on the teeth too,
Whisky, gin, brandy and ginger.

PLEASURES OF READING

Aged ten or so, I read *The Well of Loneliness*
(How did it enter the house?).
The book left an impression on me
Both indelible and indecipherable.

Aged forty, I reread *The Well of Loneliness*
And could not recognize it.
Somewhere there must be another book,
The Well of Loneliness I read at ten or so.

ESCAPISM

"That was a miserable poem you wrote about
The Black Country," said an old W.E.A. faithful
In Cradley Heath. "It's cheering up we need."
At the next meeting I tried to put him right
On this central literary issue.

Not helped by recalling that in the Twenties
And later our staple diet was *Red Letter*
And Ethel M. Dell and *Old Moore's Almanac*,

And that if you can escape for a moment
And a moment's escape is all you can manage,
No one has the right to forbid you.

34

TEMPLE BALSALL

"That splendid family
. . . their farm where I could be
'Really myself' . . ." (Philip Larkin)

The most handsome of my English uncles,
The most graceful of my aunts,
And certainly my healthiest cousins—

Brother and sister. In a childish way
I was in love with them both, but
More with her. A tall long-legged country
Beauty, and the country to play in—
For them the whole year round, for me
A week or so in summer, always summer.

The sun shone till supper-time.
The bulls were bovine, the cows benign,
The hens stepped high. How sweet we smelt
After the pigs! I don't remember
Any streets at all.

My uncle died. His wife quietly dropped
Us, as if we had somehow failed her.
What happened to Bill I can't say.
Peggy married, and died five years ago.

1,000 USEFUL THINGS TO DO
ABOUT THE HOUSE

How creative we were in those days!
We made things out of nothing
With our own hands.

In a week of evenings, for instance,
Several miles of cork-wool . . . Enough
Papier-mâché bowls to stock the V & A . . .
Trays made from melted gramophone records
Sufficient to equip Joe Lyons . . .

Now people sit and watch television.
Which is often quite instructive—
You can even listen to talks about the
Conspicuous creativity of the old days.

PREPARING FOR LIFE

Inclined to pedagogy, my favourite pursuit
(Indeed I conceived it a duty) lay in the
Education of my young sister by means of
A small blackboard and an overbearing manner.

It was not that my sister was unteachable,
Rather my methodology was out of date.
The lesson always ended with the class in tears
And the teacher summoned before God the Father.

WHATEVER SEX WAS

It was the two sisters next door
Quarrelling over their husband, or
Their drunken husband punching them.

It was the trouble that some woman
Was in, a mysterious trouble that
Could only be talked of in whispers.

It was the man who frightened my
Little sister, and whom my father
Searched the streets for, for hours.

Or the man who got angry with me
In a public lavatory, and followed me
Into the street with inexplicable curses.

It was men fighting outside the Palais.
It was crying, or it was silence.
Whatever sex was, it was another enemy.

A GRAND NIGHT

When the film *Tell England* came
To Leamington, my father said,
"That's about Gallipoli—I was there.
I'll call and see the manager . . ."

Before the first showing, the manager
Announced that "a local resident . . ." etc.
And there was my father on the stage
With a message to the troops from Sir Somebody
Exhorting, condoling or congratulating.
But he was shy, so the manager
Read it out, while he fidgeted.
Then the lights went off, and I thought
I'd lost my father.
The Expedition's casualty rate was 50%.

But it was a grand night,
With free tickets for the two of us.

BAD DAY

Talking of sticking her head in the gas oven;
Humming "There are many, sad and dreary";
Putting out bread and a basin of dripping.

A DIFFERENCE

To drown yourself in the cut
You would have to loathe yourself.
A person with any self-respect
Made use of the river. The town
Was named after the river.

EUPHEMISMS

After the main entry in clinical Latin and Greek
Which I got by heart in order to dazzle my schoolmates,
The Certificate abruptly changed its tone and remarked
That a Contributory Cause of Death was Septic Teeth.

The oddest thing, however, was to find that the Deceased
Was known as George Roderick. Perhaps this was clinical
Language too. No one ever called him anything but Mick.

INSURANCE

One spot of cheer in the Midlands gloom
Was our Dublin uncle
Who sent us shamrock each St Patrick's Day
And ebullient letters
On paper headed THE PHOENIX ASSURANCE COMPANY LTD.
He was the family success
(His photograph looks like Mickey Rooney
He could sign his name in careful Gaelic)
He moved in the corridors of power.

He came across for his brother's funeral
Pensively noting the widow and orphans at the graveside.
Something had to be said about our insurance.

He had borrowed, he intimated, the company's notepaper.
Faith, he worked there, he was a janitor there
He moved in the corridors.

Romantic Ireland was dead and gone.

THE LODGER

Our Council house would be gone as well
Unless we found a way to pay the rent.

We took a lodger, a large schoolteacher
Saving up to buy a house and marry,
His talk was all of saving.

And then his fiancée, a large girl,
Took to staying with him at weekends,
In what was once the parental bed.

It wasn't that we thought it sinful
Exactly (they were going steady),
But a slight malaise infected the house.
Perhaps it was fear of a bad name,
Or a sense of being diddled.
He was only paying rent for one.

No more lodgers, said my mother,
As the couple left for their honeymoon.

IRON HORSE

It must be admitted that Granpa
Never had a day's illness in his life
Till the time he went to the station
To see a niece off.

As the train swept in, he fell to the ground
Dead. The relicts considered the idea
Of suing the Great Western Railway for
Creating an excessive wind with fatal results,
But abandoned it.

The Bath chair went back to the owners.

THE EXCEPTION

Granpa was a sturdy exception.
Sickness too was different in those days,
People tended to die of it.

My father might be said to have invented
Lung cancer (and without benefit of smoking).

They were carried off one after another.
Such contraction of the family circle!

We noted, my sister and I, that flesh
Was weaker than the couch-grass in the yard.
It seemed hardly worth continuing with school.

GERIATRICS

I got on well with Granma.
Ours was the prescriptive relationship:
We used to play crib for hours, she gave me sweets,
She defended me, her I failed to defend.

It didn't worry me that she was getting
Troublesome. If she wandered in her mind a little,
So did I. Her husband was dead,
So was my father. The house had to be vacated.

We couldn't look after her, we were going
To look after a troublesome old man
Who at least had a house we could live in.
My eldest aunt declined to take her.

She would have to go to the Workhouse.
The worst thing was, they told her
She was going to a nursing home for a while.
They even ordered a car.

She had to be pushed into it.
As the car was moving off, I heard her
Shout with a dreadful new voice:
"I know where you're sending me,
You're sending me to the Workhouse!"

She was found to be deranged on arrival,
And they sent her on to another place.
So she didn't go to the Workhouse after all.
She died soon after.

EARLY THERAPY

Granma doddered a bit,
But she was my friend.
Perhaps it had to be done,
Did it have to be done like that?

It started me writing poems,
Unpleasant and enigmatic,
Which quite rightly no one liked,
But were thought to be "modern".

IT IS POETRY

As Leverkühn began his last address
To the cultivated ladies and gentlemen
There assembled,
They were highly bewildered.

Till one of them cried,
"Why, it is poetry! One is hearing poetry!"
Thus relieving them all immensely.

But not for long—
As the composer's friend noted—
Alas, not for long did one think so!
They were hearing about damnation.

It sent the speaker mad.
The listeners it sent home indignant.
They had expected an artistic soirée.

SCHOLARSHIP BOYS

How docile the lower orders were
In those days! Having done
Unexpectedly well in the School Cert,
I was advised by the headmaster to leave school
At once and get a job before they found
A mistake in the examination results.

And I almost did.

ALWAYS LEARNING

The gym teacher was big, handsome and
Dashing. He pronounced *tooth* as *tuth*
And *food* as *fud*, which much intrigued us.
He talked of rugger like a lover,
And rode a motorbike, big, handsome
And dashing, which we much admired.

He broke a leg in an accident
On his bike, and couldn't perform
The exercises he required of us.
He described them in words, like an elegy.
A lovely man! We groaned twice over,
For ourselves, and our disabled hero.

The months went by, he ceased to limp, but
In the gym was still the thwarted cripple.
We groaned for our sweating selves alone.
Do as I say, not as I do:
We had gained in worldly wisdom,
We had lost an admiration.

CURTAINS

If you wanted to know what you did
Last week, you asked the neighbours.

A twitching of meat-safe curtains—
Whole streets alive with tiny movements.

The nearest to privacy that I recall
Was found in close-set Council housing.

IN COLD BLOOD

The book I am reading describes how
Two young men on their way to a multiple murder
Are "chomping on two and a half sticks of Doublemint."

A sense of superiority stirs in me.
In my youth at least I had no truck with chewing gum,
Unappetizing, vulgar and embarrassing.
I once got the stuff stuck in my hair.

True, I planned a couple of murders.
But they were just, and moreover
Circumstance prevented their commission.

WEREN'T THERE ANY WINDOWS?

So my mother went to keep house for an old man,
A tyrant and a hypochondriac.
If he couldn't get what he wanted by shouting,
He got it by weeping.

He claimed he couldn't walk six yards to the lavatory.
"He killed his wife," the neighbours warned,
"He will kill your mother."

I resolved to get in first.
(Perhaps if I refused to fetch him his bucket
His bladder would burst?)

Then he became truly ill.
And one night the growth in his bowels burst,
And he died.

The stench was unexampled. My sister and I
Sat up till dawn with handkerchiefs round our mouths.
Later the fumigators came and sealed off the room,
And we packed our bags again.

A STEP UP

The next one my mother kept house for
Was a good deal more civilized.
He was headmaster of the school I went to.

He said he would be a father to me,
He said it several times with emotion.
His subject was English.

He taught me to drive his car from a nearby garage
And leave it outside the house in the mornings.

My mother fell ill and had to go to hospital.
My sister took his boiled eggs to the headmaster
In the mornings, and often dropped them
At his feet. She wasn't at home with headmasters.

My mother went on being ill,
And he decided to marry the daughter of a
Prominent and well-to-do local citizen.

Alone in a classroom he told me
Of *Romeo and Juliet*,
Then fell into a dream, while I sat there
Embarrassed.

He lost a family but gained a wife.
Some years later he died without issue.

SAID THE STRAW

"It's the last camel," said the straw,
"The last camel that breaks our backs."

"Consider the lilies," he said,
"How they toil in the fields.
Six days they labour,
On Sunday they wear their best clothes."

"Ask why the violet sickened,
The pale primrose died unmarried,
And the daisy lies in chains,"
He said, "All grass is flesh."

"But let us hear no more,"
So said the straw,
"About the sorrows of the camel
With its huge and heavy feet."

A MUCH LATER CONVERSATION

"Your father—
Did he die in error?"

Well, I suppose you could say that.
He was laid up for several months,
Then they said he was well, and
He went back to work. The next year
He was ill again, and this time he died—

"Yes, but what I mean is—"

Well, a widow's pension wasn't much.
We put it to them that getting gassed
In France had buggered up his lungs.
But the War Office wouldn't wear it,
They observed that the war had been over
For some time . . .

"I'm sorry, but I didn't mean—"

Oh yes, we had a priest in,
The first we'd ever seen at close quarters.
He gabbled in Latin,
And no one could understand him.
But at least—

"I'm sorry, but you've misunderstood me.
I was only asking
Did your father die in Eire?"

No, he died in England.
But you're right, it may have been a mistake.

KNIVES

Sheath-knives fascinated me
(Less than guns, but they were out of reach).
I owned several over the years, horn-handled,
Sheaths so stiff you could hardly pull the knife out,
And blades you could never sharpen.

On one occasion, having failed
To pierce the skin of my breast,
I turned to sharpening my pencils.
The knife wouldn't even harm a pencil—
I had to laugh.

A BOOKISH BOY

On a later and more earnest occasion
I had recourse to literature.

In this novel a youngster
Rolled in the dew on the grass and
Went to bed and caught consumption
And died.

I was taken with the dignity of it.

There being no dew available
I soaked my pyjamas under the kitchen tap
And went to bed. After a foul night
I arose from a bed of steam
Exhausted but essentially undamaged.

Plainly my mother suspected an accident,
She was too considerate to press the point.

THE LITERARY LIFE

"Poets in their middle years encounter much
That hurts and bruises them . . ."
                                        (Elizabeth Jennings)

True, Elizabeth. Who doesn't? But
How much worse it is in early years—

When you can't tell why you are out of step,
Or what your awful feelings have to do with.
Youth can be a kind of paranoia—you
Feel the shafts, you cannot recognize the bowmen.

Now at least we've learnt; and
Maybe even half-agree,
Knowing what we've done or failed to do.

Our middle years have given us—
Those useful things, what do they call them?—
Objective correlatives in plenty.

THE DOOM GAME

In those days warnings were delivered
In good round terms. One took them
Seriously.
(Except for the criminal elements
And then a few of us who made
The sceptic Sixth Form.)

These days warnings have grown common.
Hardly a wall without one, hardly a passerby
But bears a warning in his hand or mouth.
Warnings comprise our chief entertainment,
The direr the dearer,
On the radio, in the press,
In verse, in prose,
In literary criticism.

Yet one thing remains constant—
The high spirits of the warners, their
Confident step. Fears for the future
Have never cramped their present pleasures.

And now as then,
The ones who suffer already, or
Those who lie in the path of disaster—
Their mouths twitch, they cannot
Get the words out. Mumbling at most,
"It's the same old story," or
"You can't change human nature."

Such joyless clichés butter no asparagus.

LEARNING TO HICK AND TO HACK

"Much have I travelled in the realms of gold
  for which I thank the Paddington and Westminster
  Public Libraries . . ."   (Peter Porter)

Behind official bricks
We found the township's casual treasure.

The Public Library
Handsomely stocked and not used to excess
By the public—it was almost like
Having a library of one's own.
Without it, some of us wouldn't have lasted
Much past adolescence.
Into what strange routes it led us,
What pungent semi-understandings!

Bravo, England of the Thirties!
Your smallest dullest town enclosed alternatives
To littleness and dullness.

Only once were we betrayed—
In the Reference Section, where we signed our names
For the Loeb crib of the *Fasti* or the *Civil Wars*.
Loeb was more complete than our school editions,
And our faultless versions gave the game away.
So did our signatures
When the teacher called on the librarian.
I went on rather liking Ovid, though.

THE POETS

Wordsworth, Keats and Shelley—
How to picture what they meant then?
(Or the meaning that we lent them)
The critics do not tell me—
And I'm not eager to remember.
"The words on the page" came later,
When one could afford them
When one was stronger.

TIMES CHANGE

One never complained of being misunderstood!
That in fact was what, if ruefully, one hoped for.
To be understood would have been calamitous.
Silence, exile and cunning were our devices.

So now the public young and their blatant banners
Astonish me. Such honesty, such plain speaking!
I find I am blushing with retrospective shame.

SECOND THOUGHT

Why did I say that? It's not true.
At all events the blush soon faded.

A sort of honesty is safe now. What's safe
Becomes an easy fashion. Then begins to die.

I think of some I knew in Asia,
And their tiny squeaks of protest. A
Big cat watched them, and they knew it.

I pay a silent tribute to those brave mice.
What would they think, I wonder, of these
Jolly marchers flanked by well-bred horses?

RELIGIOUS PHASE

"Take an unsteady schoolboy, his whole sense
is an unskilful posture of defence" (Peter Levi)

It was the undefended one felt for.
On the third day
He arose from the dead and no doubt was
Well received at Heaven's gate.
He was on secondment. At no time
Was he ignorant of his state.

His ignorant bewildered mother
Was another matter.
In our street the pangs of labour
Were nearer than those of crucifixion.
Carpenters were useful, but
Every family required a mother.
The dirty end of the stick was known to us;
Nine months for a start
In an unskilful posture.

Because of the fear of Rome, we
Hadn't heard too much about her.
Our Church was run by married men;
They were minded to put her away privily.

As for those male toffs,
His ineffective entourage—
Johnny-come-latelies,
Made out of stained glass.

Difference of sex was no bar;
To an unsteady schoolboy
It could even have been a lure.

THE SOUL OF A SCHOOLBOY

A woman thrust her way into the house,
Desirous to save the soul of a schoolboy.

An obliging schoolboy, would do anything
For peace, excepting kneel in public.

But no, she would not go, she would not go,
Till crack on their knees they fell together.
His soul was lost forever.

SPORTS

Those cross-country runs!—how hateful
They were. One finished the course—
It was the only way home.

Jumping too. Light and long of leg, I
Could jump considerable heights if necessary.
They supposed that I liked it.

I told the head I couldn't jump this year,
It was my last year, my ankles were weak.
He sent me to a doctor, a rude man,
Who diagnosed a different weakness.

So off to the field. At the first jump
I sprained my ankles. The head was silent.
But thereafter, three times a week, I cycled
To the hospital, where a pretty nurse
Massaged my ankles. How content I was.

When summer came, I gave the master in charge
Of cricket to believe I had opted for tennis,
The master in charge of tennis I permitted
To assume I was playing cricket.

Thirty years later, in error, I attend
The Old Boys' Dinner as a distinguished guest.
Says the Chairman, "The School will always remember
Dennis Enright as—"
(Oh, I think, perhaps I've underestimated them)
"As a fine sportsman."

POSTSCRIPT

"What would be good for my ankles,
Nurse?—Apart of course from you."
(My faith in the medical profession
Had by this time been restored.)
"Cycling is good healthy exercise."

So we cycled, she and I, all the way
To the Shakespeare Memorial Theatre
At Stratford. Not that I went for
The exercise. I went for Shakespeare,
And I hope the nurse did too.

UGLY NECK

There seems to be a large gap
Somewhere about here.
If repression is at work
Then repression works efficiently,
In this sphere.

I don't remember learning about sex
In the school lavatories;
Though I remember the lavatories.

With a great effort I call up
Certain goings-on in the rear rows
Of the Physics class. I can't believe it.
That Welsh master was so sharp
You couldn't blow your nose
Without him glaring.

At one time or another
Some slightly special one or other—
But to kiss a girl
Would have seemed like criminal assault.
There was one called Pearl
Who would quote bits from Rosalind
In *As You Like It*, leaving me confused.
Once at a party I stepped heavily
On her hand, and was appalled.
In a strange way she seemed to like it.
I was glad to go home and study *The Prelude*.

It was homework and rugger; then
It was essays and walks to Grantchester.
Perhaps we were great Platonic lovers then.
Perhaps there is nothing to remember.

THE BIG STORE

What are you up to, Memory?
One day it is one thing
The next another.

I can see you
A shrewd and maybe shifty tradesman
With a variety of lines.
You study your customer's mood
You know what to offer him
And he takes it.

An emporium, a supermarket,
Macy's, and tucked away in a corner
The Piper's Penny Bazaar of childhood.
Yet by some trick of the light
It looks like a village store
Where the customer couldn't be cheated
And one quick glance at the shelves
Shows him the lot.

You know your business
You know ours.
You may deceive us a little
You prefer not to ruin us.
Only the mad and the dying
Have the run of the establishment.

CLASS

I can't help it, I still get mad
When people say that "class" doesn't mean
A thing, and to mention one's working-class
Origins is "inverted snobbery".

The wife of a teacher at school (she was
Mother of one of my classmates) was
Genuinely enraged when I won a scholarship.
She stopped me in the street, to tell me
(With a loudness I supposed was upper-class)
That Cambridge was not for the likes of me, nor was
Long hair, nor the verse I wrote for the school mag.

Her sentiments were precisely those of the
Working class. Unanimity on basic questions
Accounts for why we never had the revolution.

THE CURE

Plainly there was a lot to be done.
The trouble was, mere survival
Took up so much time and strength.

When I went to Cambridge
I found the ills had been diagnosed,
And correctly too.

But I wasn't too sure of the cure,
And couldn't quite believe
Things had once been so much better.

SENTIMENTAL JOURNEY

On a Sunday in 1968, on leave from Asia,
I set out to visit the house where I was born.

The town stirred with dust and papers,
Last night's vomit was scarcely dry.

It was cleaner than this in our day;
Perhaps we had less to throw away.

I found the street, a *cul-de-sac*
(Pudding-bag was what we called it).

Pakistanis stood there, one beside another,
Washing their second-hand cars.

They eyed the stranger not too kindly.
What could his business be in that *cul-de-sac*
But collecting payments on their cars?

ANCIENT FEARS

Accustomed to dropping into
Kempinski's, Baudrot and Raffles,
Ashoka, Ichi-Riki, Hoi Thien Lao,
And the harbour bars of Alexandria—

I enter the Cadena on Victoria Parade:
The fine matrons still frighten me.

LARGE MERCIES

I remember the schoolgirl under the bus,
Her bicycle lying in her blood,
And the driver in tears, saying over
And over, "I'll never drive again."

I remember too, her leg was amputated,
And when she passed her exams
The local paper announced it proudly,
And again when she married.

That means it wasn't a bad life.
No one was dragged out of bed by
Armed men. Children weren't speared
Or their brains dashed out. I don't
Remember seeing a man starve to death.

That's something we shouldn't forget—
That we don't remember things like that.

ACKNOWLEDGEMENTS

"But he has been equipped for hurdle-jumping;
  so he merely dreams of getting-on, but somehow
  not in the world's way."   (Richard Hoggart)

The completion of this book is in the first place
A tribute to my typewriter and its associate, the
Parker Pen. I must also acknowledge with thanks
The kindly guidance of memory, and the ever-patient
Encouragement of the author by his close friend,
The author, to whom he is also grateful as at once
The inspiration of his studies and the seminal impulse
For his interest in himself. My labours have been eased
By the gracious hospitality of my desk and the unfailing
Support of my chair. I am indebted to the Wandsworth
Borough Council for placing valuable space at my disposal,
To the London Electricity Board for throwing light on
The long winter evenings, and to the learned society of
The C.O.D. Without the research materials made available
By Life and Time, I should often have been at a loss.
Sincere apologies are offered to long-suffering friends
And relatives who would rather have lived in the present.
And finally I would record my appreciation of the
Grants-in-aid provided by Messrs Gordon, Haig and Watney,
And in particular my debt to the following Foundations:
Father, Mother, Midwife.

It takes a long time to learn a new language;
But one gets there in the end.

INDEX OF TITLES